EYE
OPENERS

EYE
OPENERS

LOOKING AT OUR LIVES
THROUGH TORAH LENSES

A TARGUM PRESS BOOK

First published 2007
Copyright © 2007 by Moshe Goldberger
POB 82, Staten Island, NY 10309
Tel: 718-948-2548
Www.GemsofTorah.com
ISBN 978-1-568-71-455-4

Published by:
TARGUM PRESS, INC.
22700 W. Eleven Mile Rd.
Southfield, MI 48034
E-mail: targum@targum.com
Fax: 888-298-9992
www.targum.com

Distributed by:
FELDHEIM PUBLISHERS
208 Airport Executive Park
Nanuet, NY 10954

Printing plates by Frank, Jerusalem
Printed in Israel by Chish

Dedicated by

The U.S./Israel Venture Summit

*An annual investment conference,
uniting Israel's most exciting early stage
and emerging companies with private
and institutional investors.*

Joseph Benjamin
www.youngstartup.com
(718) 447-0817

Special thanks
to an anonymous donor

CONTENTS

Seeing the Blessings

Guarding Against the Evil Eye

Sage Vision

Look to Hashem

PREFACE

A while back I was discussing with a close friend ideas for book topics. "How about writing on *ayin hara*?" he suggested. "We speak about it and we know we should avoid it at all costs, but do we really understand this Torah concept? Many can recite statements of Chazal about the evil eye, but we should study the subject on deeper levels. It's important to understand its parameters and how to stay away from potential trouble."

This book is a result of that conversation.

When I wrote *Eye Openers*, I started with understanding the power of the eyes and how to deal with the evil eye and expanded into other topics related to vision, such as seeing the good in the world and finding Hashem in everything that happens to us. This book, of course, cannot encompass every aspect of these subjects; it only scratches the surface. But it contains valuable tools for growth and success by using the power of our eyes to see the world through Torah vision.

Rashi gives three reasons why Sarah Imeinu was called Yiskah, which comes from the Hebrew word for "look" (*Bereishis* 11:29):

1. She saw things with *ruach hakodesh*, a spirit of holiness.

2. Everyone saw her beauty.

3. She was a leader, whom everyone looked up to.

What is the connection between these three reasons, and what does the third reason have to do with vision?

Rav Moshe Feinstein, *zt"l*, in *Dorash Moshe*, explains that when a person looks at others, he chooses what he will focus on and how he wants to view what he is seeing. Likewise, when others are looking at us, we hope that they will see the good within us.

Sarah saw the good in everyone and everything. When she looked at people, she saw their inner potential. And when others looked at her, and saw how she acted and presented herself, they did not see her outer beauty; they were seeing the beauty of her inner essence. Finally, with her vision, Sarah saw the holy potential within herself.

All of these three "views" are what led to her becoming the great assistant leader to her husband, Avraham Avinu.

Each of us, says Rav Moshe, can and should develop the ability to always see the good in others and to enable others to see the good in us so that we merit to become leaders and to see and fulfill our unique potential.

That is the theme of this book.

MG

INTRODUCTION

The way you look at things can make all the difference. Hashem designed the world so that we would be presented with ongoing challenges in order to stimulate our growth. The story, or meaning, that we attach to these challenges will determine whether or not we change in a positive way.

Some people use the challenging events in their lives as excuses not to grow. They choose to feel rejected, lonely, or helpless. They view themselves as failures. Others understand that these events represent the possibilities of what they can accomplish. They realize that they are being provided with great opportunities to grow, develop, and succeed.

How can we get the most out of our challenges?

Imagine what it is like to put on glasses for the first time. Suddenly, everything comes into focus. That which was blurry and hard to see has now become crystal clear.

Similarly, you can create your own set of "spiritual

glasses." You can learn how to sharpen your focus by seeing the events that happen to you through Torah guidelines. When you put on these glasses, suddenly you see opportunities all around you and your choices become crystal clear. Just as eyeglasses are merely letting you see what was there all the time, when you learn how to see things with clarity, you realize that all of the brilliant detail and insight was actually present all along. You just needed the right glasses with which to see it. In this way, the eyes serve as glasses for the soul, and the Torah of Hashem and the insights of our Sages are the lenses through which one must view every aspect of life.

In the chapters that follow, you will learn how to create your own set of spiritual glasses. Then you will be able to discover and utilize the opportunities that Hashem has hidden in everything that happens to you in order to succeed in life.

Who Desires Life?

Mi ha'ish hechafetz chaim oheiv yamim liros tov... — Who desires life? Who loves days [and desires] to see good?...

(*Tehillim* 34:13)

Live with the attitude, ambition, and determination to see the good — and Hashem will make it happen! As our Sages teach, "On the path one is determined to go, Hashem will lead him" (*Makkos* 10b).

CHANGING
YOUR
OUTLOOK

Chapter 1

EVERYTHING HASHEM DOES IS FOR GOOD

Hashem is good to all; His mercies are on all His works.

(*Tehillim* 145:9)

Hashem created this world in order to bestow goodness and kindness on His creations, as the Gemara teaches us, "Everything Hashem does is for good" (*Berachos* 60b). The way in which He designed and runs the world is always "win-win" for all — He has unlimited resources with plenty to go around to fulfill everyone's needs.

All eyes hope to You, and You provide them their food in its proper time.

(Ibid., 15)

Not only does Hashem bestow unlimited good upon all of His creations, but by developing this outlook, we cause Hashem to make everything even more beneficial for us. We can actually change our experience by choosing to change our thoughts and perspective.

When you look at a situation and tell yourself, "Everything Hashem does is for good," that very thought causes Hashem to bring you good, as the *pasuk* says, "Blessed is a person who trusts in Hashem, and Hashem will fulfill his trust" (*Yirmeyahu* 17:7). The commentators explain that the more one trusts in Him, the more He will provide His guidance and help.

Thus, you can generate more abundance from Hashem by your positive vision. When you change the way you see the world, the world you see will adjust so that you can receive more of Hashem's bounty. By choosing how you will think and deciding to have a positive attitude, you will experience more benefits. If you envision a positive situation and pray for Hashem's help, it will happen.

When Everything Seems to Go Wrong

Rabbi Akiva was accustomed to saying, "Everything Hashem does is for good." Once, Rabbi Akiva was traveling with a donkey, a rooster, and a candle. When night came, he couldn't find lodging in the nearby village and had to sleep outside in a field. A wind came and blew out his candle, a wild cat ate his rooster, and a lion came and ate his donkey. Rabbi Akiva's reaction was "Everything Hashem does is for good."

That night, a regiment of soldiers came and took the entire town captive while Rabbi Akiva was spared. When Rabbi Akiva realized what happened, he said, "Didn't I say that everything that Hashem does is for good?" If Rabbi Akiva had had the candle, rooster, or donkey, he would have been seen or heard and they might have captured him, too.

(*Berachos* 60b)

When everything seems to be going wrong, realize that Hashem is working hard (so to speak) to help you. Remember: Everything Hashem does is for good!

Chapter 2

SEEING THE GOOD

Hashem saw that the light was good.

(Bereishis 1:4)

R ight here, writes Rav Avigdor Miller (*The Beginning*, p. 20), we encounter the following major Torah principle: "We need to emulate Hashem's ways to fulfill the obligation to 'walk in His ways' (*Devarim* 28:9)." Hashem "saw that the light was good"; so, too, we should see the good in everything. It is not enough just to *know* that everything Hashem does is for good. We need to *see* the good — to consider the benefits, plan and purpose, wisdom, and goodness in every situation.

When we choose to develop the habit of seeing the good in every situation, we learn to appreciate everything Hashem has provided for us, we become more productive, and we enjoy life more.

Imagine that you are waiting in an airport when you receive a message that your flight was delayed for two hours due to mechanical problems. What is your reaction? You can grumble and complain and then spend the next two hours fuming, or you can say: "*Gam zu l'tovah!* This must be for my benefit!"

Then you can consider: How can I benefit from the situation? How can I utilize the next two hours in the most productive manner?

You can take the opportunity to enjoy some much needed relaxation. You can find a private corner where you can catch up on some of your work or study Torah. Maybe you can even take a nap. And, of course, don't forget to thank Hashem for arranging this pleasant interlude!

In this way, you can turn a seemingly difficult situation into one of growth.

The Right Outlook

The difference between *oneg* (ענג) pleasure, and *nega* (נגע), a plague of leprosy, is where we place the letter *ayin* (also the Hebrew word for "eye"). If the *ayin* is in the beginning — if you choose to view things in a positive light — then any situation can be elevated and transformed into a pleasure (*Sfas Emes*).

Chapter 3

FACING
CHALLENGES

In the previous chapters, we learned that any situation can be turned into an opportunity for growth and success. We can do this by looking for the good even in the most difficult situation.

This is easier said than done. A flight delay can be frustrating, but it isn't hard to accept that we can find the good in it. But how can we see the good in more challenging situations?

Everyone experiences difficulties in their lives. It is how we view these difficulties that determines the effects they will have on us. Do events that happen to you control your choices, or do you look at challenges as a stepping-stone to achieving great levels?

There was once a man who learned that he had a disease that could cause blindness within six months. He became depressed and as a result suffered terribly. He let negative thoughts blind him to the truth that his life could still have meaning and he could still accomplish great things in so many areas. If he would have tried to look at his situation in a positive light, he would have realized that there are many ways of "seeing." There have been people in history who lost their sight, but they learned to "see" even better with their hearts. These were people who, because of their positive outlook despite their difficult circumstances, achieved great levels.

This brings us to an incredible Torah lesson regarding one of the greatest personalities in history, Yitzchak Avinu. The Torah tells us that when he became old, "his eyes became dim" (*Bereishis* 27:1). Later we learn how his younger son, Yaakov, was able to step in and receive the greatest blessing in history because Yitzchak thought that he was giving the *berachah* to the eldest, Esav. Imagine what could have happened if Yitzchak would not have been blind and Esav would have received the blessings rather than Yaakov! Rav Avigdor Miller explains (*The Beginning*, p. 420) that we learn from this that seeing can sometimes be worse than blindness, because the eyes can deceive the mind.

At times it appears that there is no hope, that there is no way to succeed and you are tempted to give up. But every situation can be turned around with Hashem's help to become an opportunity for growth and success.

Don't Give Up

There is a story of an individual who wanted to start a radio station for which he needed a million dollars of seed funding. He was turned down by thirty-two potential investors. Finally, after presentation 33, a banker agreed to the loan. Now the group has more than fifty stations around the country. After thirty failures, or even twenty, or even ten, most people might have given up. But this man did not let a negative outlook get in the way of what he wanted to achieve.

Not everyone sees things your way, but with persistence and Hashem's help, there is no limit to what you can accomplish, as *Mishlei* teaches, "A righteous person may fall seven times, but he keeps getting up" (*Mishlei* 24:16).

Chapter 4

THE CHALLENGE OF CHILD-REARING

Let us look at one of the challenges in life: child-rearing. When children behave as they should, we can easily see the good in this challenge. That is when we experience *nachas* and reap the reward of our efforts. But what about the rest of the time? What about the sleepless nights and all the hard work and effort in order to provide for them, both physically and spiritually? At those times, it is harder to consider how this challenge benefits us.

In truth, the challenge of child-raising brings immeasurable benefits. Here are just a few:

❖ *You become a better person.* Children help you improve your character and become a better person. The challenge of child-rearing makes you more patient, accepting, tolerant, and flexible. It teaches you to be more generous and joyful. You become more giving, not only to your children, but also to everyone else around you.

❖ *You learn to accept yourself for who you are.* Hashem gives children the parents they need in order to become the people they are supposed to become. You don't need to try to be someone else with children, because that is not what they need. Only when you accept yourself for who you are and learn to be your best can you be the best parent for your child.

❖ *You gain new perspectives.* As children grow up and learn about the world around them, they ask questions: Why is the sky blue? How hot is the sun? Why are babies so small? Their questions open your eyes and spur you to think about what is important in life. They teach you to pay attention and treasure the moments of your life. As you watch a child grow, you start to realize that Hashem has sent this child into your life to open your eyes. Children help us slow down, think more, talk less, and learn to pay attention. In other words, children teach you to be humble.

Part of the challenge of child-rearing is what is called "tough love." When a child is going through a difficult time, or when he is misbehaving, it is important to remember that he needs your love and understanding even more. At the same time, realize that he needs your guidance, so that he will not make the same mistakes and will learn good habits that will lead him to success in life. He needs you to teach him to make the right choices — how to take responsibility for his actions and not to make excuses if he has done something wrong.

Remember: Each child is the greatest of gifts from Hashem. Let us treasure that gift.

Instead of looking for the difficulty in every opportunity, look for the opportunity in every difficulty!

Chapter 5

APPRECIATING EACH OTHER'S DIFFERENCES

No two people see the same thing the same way. Just as no two people look alike, so, too, no two people think alike (*Sanhedrin* 38a).

When you look at someone, do you see him as an individual with unique tastes and viewpoints, or do you assume that he is just like you? If you think everyone is like you, you can be sure that you are not really "seeing" them!

A writer learns to develop the skill of picturing the effects that his words will have on his readers. In order to draw them into his story, he has to connect with them and earn their trust. To make his characters believable, he must make it a habit to observe how people react in different circumstances. He must learn to be observant of the smallest details and then use what he learns to connect with his readers. If we would study people the way a writer does, we couldn't help but learn to appreciate others' viewpoints and become more selfless, understanding, and giving.

You may have heard the famous story of Rabbi Akiva's daughter and the snake (*Shabbos* 156b). The stargazers came to Rabbi Akiva and told him that his daughter would perish from a snakebite on the day of her wedding. On that day, she stuck her hairpin into a wall, killing the snake. The following morning, she discovered the snake with a pin through its eye.

Rabbi Akiva asked her, "What special act did you perform yesterday?"

She said, "A pauper came to the door, but everyone was busy with the party and ignored him. I noticed him and took my portion of food and gave it to him."

Rabbi Akiva said, "You have a done a great mitzvah. *Tzedakah tatzil mimaves* — Charity saves from death! In the merit of your kind act, you were saved from the snake."

If you take a closer look at this Talmudic story, you will notice an eye-opening word. It says: "She stuck her hairpin into the *eye* of the snake." Why did Hashem cause her to be saved in this way?

It was a measure-for-measure reward: since she

used her eyes to notice the plight of the pauper, she was spared by putting a pin through the eye of the snake.

It is interesting to note that this occurred on her wedding day. The greatest test of marriage is learning to focus on the other person. The whole purpose of marriage is to notice the needs of the other spouse and to try to fulfill them. Through this, we become a more giving person and a better Jew. This is the test of marriage, which Rabbi Akiva's daughter passed with flying colors.

The Key to Wisdom

There was a governor who made it a practice to go out, one day here, one day there, to mingle with his people and perform different jobs. When asked why he did this, he said that he wanted to walk in the shoes of those whom he represented in order to understand them better and learn their viewpoints.

The governor understood the benefits of learning the perspectives of diverse people who had seen things he would never see. By going out and working with the people, he was able to be a better, more effective leader.

Who is wise? One who learns from every person.

(*Avos* 4:1)

Chapter 6

LOOKING AHEAD

Who is wise? One who sees what can develop.

(*Tamid* 32a)

It would be foolish to set out on a trip without considering how you are going to get there. If you don't plan your route before you start, you will never reach your destination. Similarly, it is impossible to achieve anything in life without setting goals and thinking about how you will accomplish them.

Hashem created us with eyes that can be used to look ahead for a purpose. Just as it is advisable to look ahead to see up and down the block before walking down a street, so too it pays to look ahead in every area of life.

Let's say you are looking for a job. What would give you a better chance of getting the position you want?

First, you would research the company where you are applying to learn what kind of person they want to fill that position. On the day of the interview you would dress and act the part of a person in that role. Even if you don't yet have all of the qualifications, if you act like the right person for the job, you have a better chance of getting it. Eventually you will learn all you need to know to do the job.

Similarly, if you imagine that you have become a great Torah scholar, you can boost yourself onto an upward track. You will be more committed and determined to achieve when you see the possibility of what you can become. Place yourself, emotionally, mentally, and physically, in the location you desire to be and you will find it easier to elevate yourself to that level.

> Looking ahead is like a place marker to get you there. Before you go anywhere, imagine that you have already arrived.

INNER VISION

Chapter 7

THE KEY TO GROWTH

The key to growth is seeing yourself as who you really are and envisioning who you can become. When you truly know yourself, you can take steps to change and grow.

In this section, we will learn how to "see" ourselves and figure out what we can become. We will discuss what steps we can take to change so that we will put ourselves on the path to fulfilling our potential.

In order to learn who you are, ask yourself the following questions:

- ❖ What is my job in life?

- ❖ What do I enjoy doing?

- ❖ What is my motivation behind my actions — can I do everything I do as a service to Hashem?

- ❖ How can I make a lasting impact on my life?

❖ What changes do I need to make in my life in order to succeed?

❖ Do I learn from my mistakes?

In this section we will look inward with our inner vision to learn about ourselves and strive to answer these questions.

Who is wise? One who learns from every person.

(Avos 4:1)

Don't miss the opportunity to "learn" from yourself — to learn from your mistakes and grow from them.

Chapter 8

FINDING YOUR STORY

I have placed life and death before you... Choose life.
(*Devarim* 30:19)

O ur purpose in life is to "choose life" — to make the choice to do good. Thus, Hashem surrounds us with challenges in order to give us the opportunity to make the right choices. In other words, we need to "see" through the challenges to discover the right path for us to take — the path to good. When people are faced with difficult challenges, they are forced to confront their choices as they strive to grow.

How do we know what is the right choice? In order to be able to make the right choices, it is essential to figure out "*mah chovaso b'olamo* — what is my obligation in the world Hashem designed for me?" (*Mesilas Yesharim*, ch. 1).

The first step to learning our place in life is to look back at all of our experiences and the events that happened to us and think about how we reacted to those experiences — how we felt and what we did. We must also consider which experiences brought us closer to Hashem — when did we make the right choices that brought us to higher levels in our *avodas Hashem*? When we add together all of these visions, we can form a composite picture, or story, of who we are.

Of course, we cannot know exactly how all of our experiences fit together. Only Hashem, who is running the show, truly knows how the events in our life add up. However, by looking at our past experiences as challenges to perfect ourselves, we can have some idea of what it is we are meant to accomplish in this world.

As the story of your life takes shape, it develops into a program for your own personal growth. This program should be made up of a combination of challenge, excitement, meaning, and fulfillment.

When you "find your story" and begin to understand who you are, you may find that you have already developed the qualities you need to continue on your mission. You may see that you still have a lot to learn in order to accomplish what you need to do. Or you may discover that you have been going in the wrong direction all along. This does not mean that all is lost. No matter which direction you are headed now, you can always shift your course.

If you have been going in the wrong direction or you still have to develop the qualities you need to accomplish your mission, then the challenge is to truly believe that you can change. When you realize that you are on the right path, you can bear all the challenges along the road and persist to make it work. When you see your goals with clarity, you can turn all of your weaknesses into strengths.

Every moment is a chance to make a new choice. Every situation contains a golden mitzvah opportunity that you can mine to transform it into an eternal acquisition of perfection.

Golden Opportunities
Be thankful even for those who cause you some annoyance — they, too, are helping you learn and grow. One who is truly wise learns from *every* person.

Chapter 9

A GOOD EYE

[Rabbi Yochanan ben Zakkai] said to [his five disciples]:
Go out and see, which is the best path to which a person
should cling? Rabbi Eliezer said: A good eye. Rabbi
Yehoshua said: A good friend. Rabbi Yosei said: A good
neighbor. Rabbi Shimon said: One who considers the
outcome of a deed. Rabbi Elazar said: A good heart...

(*Avos* 2:13)

Why does this *mishnah* give five different answers to the question of how to live?

Every person is unique, just as the five fingers on your hand are each a different size and shape. Every person has his own viewpoints, character traits, and abilities that make him different from everyone else in the world. These unique abilities define his mission and the purpose for which he was created. Hashem gives each person his unique situation to fit his task in life — like a well-made glove tailored to fit one's hand (*Berachos* 43b).

A Good Eye

As you write the story of your life, remember that your place in this world is unique and no one else can fulfill your mission. This is why it is essential to learn your purpose in life — if you don't fulfill it, no one else can.

If that is true, why does the *mishnah* insist, "Go out and see, which is the best path to which a person should cling"? If each person has a unique mission that only he can fulfill, why does he need to go out and search for it? Wouldn't it be so much better if he received a direct communication from Hashem saying, "This is what you are here for..."?

We are meant to search for our path, because, as our Sages teach, "On the path one is determined to go, he will be led" (*Makkos* 10b). We must show Hashem that we want to find our path and only then will He lead us to it.

The first answer in the *mishnah* above is "A good eye." Your slim notion or slight urge to follow a certain path can only mature into a full vision if you follow it with a "good eye."

How do we define a "good eye"? Rambam says that it means being satisfied with one's lot. Rabbeinu Yonah interprets it as rejoicing with one's portion. It is not enough to realize one's mission in life — one must embark on his true path with joy and enthusiasm. Only then will one succeed to the fullest extent.

David HaMelech davened to Hashem, "I asked G-d for one constant request...: to dwell in the House of Hashem all the days of my life, to view the pleasantness of Hashem..." (*Tehillim* 27:4). It is not enough to dwell in the House of Hashem — to follow in the right path and serve Hashem. One must also be able to "view the pleasantness of Hashem" — to take pleasure from following the right path.

We pray to Hashem not only to grant us the merit to learn His Torah — but to grant us *our portion* of His Torah.

Chapter 10
DIRECT YOUR GAZE

If you gaze at three things, you will be protected from sin: Know where you came from, where you are going, and before Whom you will have to give an accounting.

(Avos 3:1)

As we reflect on what to do with our life, we must focus on the "eye that sees everything we do" (*Avos* 2:1) and know that we will all stand judgment eventually and be held accountable for our choices. Thus we need to know where we are ultimately headed to ensure that when our day of judgment comes, we will have accomplished worthwhile goals. We do not want to squander our time here.

Knowing where we are headed makes all the difference while we struggle with questions and issues that crop up. We need to explore who we are and what we need to achieve:

❖ When should we accept our lot and stop pushing for change?

❖ How do we balance internal growth with external achievements?

❖ How do we know when it is time to change our environment and when we need to change ourselves?

We can only deal with our issues if we know clearly in which direction we should be headed. Then we will be on our way to true growth and success.

A Prayer for Wisdom
> *Tehillim* teaches us this prayer for wisdom:
>
> *Teach us to count our days properly, so that we will develop a heart of wisdom.*
>
> (*Tehillim* 90:12)

Chapter 11

THINK MORE,
SAY LESS

In the previous chapters, we learned that in order to succeed you need to discover and define your purpose in life. This will enable you to accomplish more than you thought possible. When you define clearly what is your purpose, you will be spurred to channel all of your desires and efforts onto the path that will lead to achieving it. *Mesilas Yesharim* teaches that when you develop a clear picture of your purpose in this world, when you truly "see" your purpose, life will never be the same again — when you know where you are headed and what you desire to accomplish, everything suddenly has meaning. In the next few chapters, we will learn what are the steps we need to take in order to define that purpose.

The first step is to give yourself time to reflect and think. To this purpose, the Mishnah gives good advice:

אמר מעט — *Say little.*

(*Avos* 1:14)

Why is "saying little" so important for reflecting on what we need to accomplish?

Rav Dovid Aharon, *shlita*, explains that the three words for "word" in Hebrew demonstrate limitation:

1. *Milah* (מלה) — the literal translation is to "cut off," as when used for *bris milah*. Words serve as labels that cut reality into distinct pieces.

2. *Teivah* (תיבה) — this word also means "box." Words put reality into specific containers.

3. *Davar* (דבר) — literally, "thing." Words take reality and turn it into specific items.

The Sages teach: "Silence is a fence for wisdom" (*Avos* 3:13). If we want to learn our purpose in life, we have to give ourselves a chance to think. If we use too many words, we may limit our understanding of our life story.

Rav Aharon illustrates this idea with the Talmudic explanation (*Niddah* 30b) that an angel taps a person on his mouth before birth, causing him to forget his learning. Why does he tap the mouth? Why doesn't he give the baby a tap on the head? Isn't the head the center of wisdom?

The Maharal explains that our speech can limit our

understanding. By tapping the baby on the mouth, the angel is limiting the baby's understanding of the Torah so that he can forget it in order to learn it anew.

When you are exploring your life's purpose, what your mission is in life, you must allow yourself the opportunity to reflect and consider what you need to do. Only then can you define and articulate your purpose.

The Most Productive Hour of the Day

An hour of thinking and planning can save you many hours of unproductive work. The time you set aside for reflection may be your most productive hour of the day.

Chapter 12

FINDING YOUR DREAM

Have you ever asked yourself, "What should I do with my life?" — or perhaps the question should be: How many times have you asked yourself this question? This question is related to figuring out "Who am I?" and "Where do I belong?" There is a connection between who you are and what you do. In order to find out who you are, you need to consider what you like to do.

Hashem created each individual with unique gifts to develop and share with the world (*Berachos* 43b). Some people like to be around others most of the time. Others enjoy being alone. Some like adventure, while others like things to stay on an even keel. Some enjoy working with children, and some have a special affinity with the elderly. Take the time to consider: What is your *neshamah* saying to you? What makes your soul sing?

Why is it so important to do something you enjoy? Why can't a person simply choose to do something that can make him wealthy? Why not get rich first and then fulfill one's personal dreams in life?

When a person's only motivation in choosing what to do with his life is to get rich, he will never reach his goals. Someone whose goal is to be wealthy will never feel that he has achieved it. He will always feel that he does not have enough yet.

What we do affects our mind-set and approach to life. It's not only who we are that's important — it's also what we do, because that influences what we become. Money is not meant to be the path to freedom. It is only meant to be a tool to be utilized as we discipline ourselves to live within our means. A sense of purpose and meaning in one's work will bring a feeling of satisfaction that is equal to, or even greater than, a large income.

Let us keep in mind that Hashem always provides for us. He never has any shortages. Make it your goal to enjoy what you do so that you will be able to serve Hashem better — and let Hashem take care of the rest!

Life Scenery
A truck driver was asked why he liked his job. "Because," he answered, "the view changes with every mile!"

Chapter 13

LOVE YOUR WORK

Shemayah says: Love work...

(Avos 1:10)

Do you know someone who can't wait to get to work? He jumps out of bed and prepares for his workday with a smile and a bounce in his step. He davens happily with the early minyan, looking forward to his day.

Then there are those who struggle to drag themselves out of bed in the morning. They face their day with dread. They show up at the late minyan and make it to work only just in time. Their unhappiness at work leaves them feeling discouraged and unmotivated.

According to the Mishnah, we should be like the man who loves work. Someone who does not find fulfillment and happiness in what he is doing cannot serve Hashem properly. Our Sages teach us (*Sanhedrin* 99b) that Hashem created us to work hard — we cannot truly achieve anything if we don't work for it. But this does not mean that we should not enjoy our work. We should feel fulfilled and proud of what we do. Our work should help us serve Hashem somehow.

In the previous chapter, we said that one way to love your work is to do something you enjoy doing. This is a clue to what you should do with your life, and in this way you will find joy and fulfillment. Another aspect to consider is that we feel fulfilled in our work when we are able to give to others in some capacity.

This can take many forms, from becoming a doctor who heals people to teaching Torah to children to being a gardener. Any job that gives a person meaning provides him the opportunity to help others and thus be happy.

Ask yourself: Do you connect with others on a daily basis? Is what you do helping people somehow?

It may take some focus and discipline, but just about any profession can be performed with the intention of contributing to the well-being of others — which is one of the greatest mitzvos of the Torah!

Three Ways to Serve Hashem
How do we serve Hashem?
In three ways:

1. Study His Torah.

2. Connect to Him with prayer.

3. Ask others (or think to yourself): How can I help? (When you help people for the right reasons, you are serving Hashem.)

(Based on *Avos* 1:2)

Chapter 14

FOUR STEPS TO SUCCESS

You have spent time reflecting on what your place is in life. You have thought about what you enjoy doing, and you have chosen to spend your day doing something that gives your life meaning.

Now that you have a direction in which you should be heading — your own unique path to follow — you may realize that you will have to make some changes in order to succeed. The Mishnah (*Avos* 4:1) teaches us a four-step formula for succeeding in life:

1. Learn from others and acquire wisdom.

2. Conquer your temptations and learn self-control.

3. Rejoice with your portion and achieve true wealth.

4. Honor others and you will receive honor.

These four areas involve important qualities that

you will need in order to accomplish your life mission: wisdom, self-control, contentment and joy, and respect. With these traits one can improve oneself and set himself on the right path. In the next chapters we will explore these qualities.

Keys to Growth
The keys to change are in your hands!

The key to wisdom is to learn from all others.
The key to strength is to conquer your inclination.
The key to wealth is to rejoice with your portion.
The key to honor is to honor others.

Chapter 15

WAYS TO WISDOM

Who is wise? One who learns from every person.
(*Avos* 4:1)

People have a natural tendency to look to other people as their yardsticks on how to act, speak, and dress. The question is: who are we learning from — who is our yardstick for success? When we are looking to others to gauge how we should act, we need to direct our gaze to righteous people who keep Torah and mitzvah values.

Learning from others brings many benefits, including:

❖ knowledge,

❖ motivation, and

❖ humility.

When we learn from others, we gain *knowledge* we did not have before. The more knowledge we have, the wiser we can be.

Also, when we look to others whom we like and respect we are *motivated* to achieve greater levels. For one thing, when we compare ourselves with others, it helps us see inside ourselves and appreciate the magnificent potential within us. This is one of the most important lessons we learn from observing others — that Hashem made each of us unique and gave each of us abilities and talents that we can develop to achieve greatness.

On the other hand, we also learn how to be *humble*, to give up our ego, in order to learn from the people around us. Even if a person teaches you one line of Torah, he deserves your respect (see *Avos* 6:3). By learning from others and showing them honor — a genuine respect for their point of view — we develop our own unique portion even more. Then we will have even more reason to rejoice with our portion.

If I am not for myself, who will be for me?

(*Avos* 1:14)

You have the ability to succeed with Hashem's help. Invest your efforts and pray to Hashem, and you will be on the road to success!

Chapter 16

SEEING THE
POTENTIAL

Who is wise? One who sees what can develop.

(Tamid 32a)

One who has acquired wisdom has the ability to "see what can develop." This not only requires wisdom, but also imagination and vision.

In order to accomplish your goals, you have to imagine yourself succeeding. In order to do this, you need vision — you need to be able to look ahead and see yourself in the place where you hope to be one day.

Something that is a mystery to most people is obvious and real to someone with the wisdom and vision to look ahead, as the *Mesilas Yesharim* says (in the Preface): "That which is well known and revealed to all, people are unaware of and they forget." In other words, that which seems to be so essential and obvious is often invisible to most people. Someone with imagination and vision can see things that are "invisible" to others. He can use his imagination to understand what can develop in the future.

Great inventors are well known for this quality. Imagine what it would be like to invent something. Take an ordinary object, such as a telephone. Consider how in the last hundred years people have come along and improved it — made it smaller, bigger, cheaper, faster, more colorful, exciting. These ideas are very simple, but until someone came and thought about it, they didn't exist yet. These ideas were born of vision. Without the vision to see the potential of things, these new and improved telephones — or even the telephone itself — could not have been invented.

Imagine

Practice expanding your vision so that you can imagine your own potential and see "what can develop."

Use your vision to imagine:

Can you invent colorful salt?

Better salt?

Cheaper salt?

Healthier salt?

Chapter 17

SERVING HASHEM WITH JOY

Every day in our morning prayers we are reminded that we must "serve Hashem with joy" (*Mizmor L'Sodah, Tehillim* 100:2). In order to serve Hashem properly and thus fulfill one's potential, one must be happy. Happiness is essential to success.

A person is happy when he knows he is doing what he is supposed to be doing. This means staying on the right path and serving Hashem. Staying balanced in your focus of serving Hashem is the most powerful way to develop a sense of wholeness and complete dedication, which in turn brings joy. If you are not happy with how your life is going, it may be a sign that you are going in the wrong direction.

Even if you are growing and advancing on the right path, sometimes life is so stressful and over-whelming that you find it difficult to be happy. It is important to find ways to relax, to set aside time in your day when you can enjoy yourself. When you re-lax, you can focus better and see your next step more clearly. Relaxing is a mitzvah when you do it in order to serve Hashem!

Here are some simple ways to lower your stress level and relax:

❖ Stop what you are doing and take five deep breaths. Feel yourself relaxing and ready to go on with your day.

❖ Take some time to think about the good in your life and to thank Hashem for it.

❖ Go outside and take a walk. Use the opportunity to thank Hashem for the beautiful world He created for you. Notice the trees lining your block and the singing birds and thank Hashem for them.

❖ Splash some water on your face. Refresh yourself and thank Hashem for the miracle of water.

❖ Phone a friend and say, "Your name popped into my head and I wanted to say hello."

❖ Say a prayer to Hashem.

Another quality that is vital to being happy and serving Hashem is one of the "steps to success" that we quoted above:

Serving Hashem with Joy

Who is wealthy? One who rejoices with his portion.

(*Avos* 4:1)

When you look at your possessions, are you thinking, "I don't have enough, I want more," or do you feel content that you have everything you need?

This, the Torah teaches, was the difference between Yaakov and Esav. When you "rejoice in your portion," you are emulating Yaakov who said, "*Yeish li kol* — I have everything!" (*Bereishis* 33:11).

"Enough" is all about attitude — it's a way of thinking, seeing, and feeling. It is the result of the vision with which you choose to view your life. You have the power to choose now to be satisfied and thankful to Hashem for His great bounty to you.

You may have heard of the businessman who wore a pinstriped suit who said: "These stripes are my jail bars." Or the one who thought he would be happy if he became rich. When he had a million dollars in his account, he saw that he was no happier than he was before. In fact, he was actually less happy than before.

We don't need a businessman to tell us this. Chazal explain that one who has one million desires two; one who has two wants to have four (Midrash, *Koheles*). Conversely, by having less, one's needs are less and thus one can be happier, because he is lacking less. One who rejoices with what he has is the one who is truly happy. One who sees the blessings in his life and feels he has enough is the one who experiences true joy. Conversely, one who is always pursuing wealth and does not feel he has enough is never happy.

Money in itself cannot bring joy. A person who is wealthy is not automatically happy. It is only when he uses his wealth as a tool to do good and serve Hashem that it brings him contentment and satisfaction.

The Lottery

If you would win the lottery and become very wealthy, how would you use your winnings? Would you use the money to secure your wealth, prestige, and job security, or to strive for more than material gain — to accomplish a greater good or to become a great, wise person? What you do with your money is what makes all the difference.

Chapter 18

SEEING THE OBVIOUS

*The eyes of a fool are focused on the end of the world,
whereas a wise person sees in front of him.*

(*Mishlei* 17:24)

Sometimes, in trying to improve ourselves, we look for a cause in which to invest our efforts. But in looking outside ourselves for a problem to solve, we miss the obvious: our own issues.

Hashem is patient — He keeps sending us challenges, waiting for us to pay attention and confront our shortcomings. When we are suffering a difficult trial, it may be a message that we need to look at our own unresolved issues rather than look outside for a new cause. A trial is sent to us to change us, to force us to focus on ourselves and what we need to be doing differently in our lives. It is up to us to be open to the change and be willing to face our issues.

Hashem's guiding hand causes everything to happen, even things that seem coincidental. The word מקרה is literally translated as "happening" or "coincidence." But there is no such thing as a coincidence. The letters of the word מקרה can thus be rearranged to become רק מה', "only from Hashem."

Everything that happens in this world, the good and the bad, comes from Hashem. Hashem not only directs the traffic, He also positions the bumps on the road!

When something happens that stops you in your tracks, whether it is a minor annoyance or a life-shattering event, know that Hashem made this happen for a reason. Instead of spinning your wheels, feeling angry or depressed, back up and ask Hashem which direction He wants you to take.

Creative Vision

We tend to gain more from the things on which we focus our attention. To achieve your goals, focus hard and fast, with solid determination, on what you desire to create.

Chapter 19

LOOKING BACK

You have discovered your place in life. You have thought about the things you most enjoy doing. You have resolved to succeed by acquiring the qualities you need to achieve greatness. You have confronted your issues and realized that you need to make changes in order to accomplish your mission in life. But making a change can be daunting. How do you make those changes?

The Torah provides a fail-safe program for change: the mitzvah of *teshuvah*, repentance.

Everyone makes mistakes. *Teshuvah* is the opportunity to erase those mistakes and move forward. Failing is challenging, but it can always be remedied with repentance. This does not mean that your mistakes serve no purpose. They can be the most valuable lessons you will ever learn to motivate you for the rest of your life.

The possibility of making mistakes and the opportunity to rectify them is what makes us human and differentiates us from the rest of creation. Hashem provides us with the privilege of free will to enable us to continuously author our own lives. We are free to make choices, and the greatest choice is to keep growing in our service of Hashem. That includes learning from our mistakes, repenting for wrongdoings, and resolving to do better in the future.

By looking *back* with a view to repentance, we can improve the way we look *ahead* to prepare ourselves for the next step.

SEEING THE
BLESSINGS

Chapter 20

THE BIG PICTURE

Your heart beats 100,000 times a day.

The sun is only a minor star among 100 billion in a galaxy which is relatively small among countless galaxies.

Thirteen billion gallons of water flow over Niagara Falls every day.

How many blades of grass are there on your lawn? Millions? Billions?

How many leaves are there on the tree in front of your house?

There is an incredible amount of abundance in this world that Hashem created just for us. Not only did He create everything with phenomenal abundance, but He also recycles everything that is not used to return eventually in a new form at a later date. The world contains a built-in vision and foresight for ongoing planning.

Even more, Hashem has arranged everything for the benefit of all involved. For example, for everything you want to sell, there is someone who wants to buy it.

For what you want to buy, there is someone looking to sell it. There is perfect balance and timing in everything that happens in this world.

The world is indeed filled with blessings. The question is, do we see and appreciate the blessings?

This is our challenge — to see if we can hold on to our vision of the big picture and realize how even the smallest creations are in place by divine order. Hashem plans everything with our best interests in mind.

There was once a survey in which people were asked what was the worst thing that ever happened to them and what was the best thing that ever happened to them. They discovered that there was an 80 percent correlation between the worst thing and the best thing. In other words, the terrible eventually turned into the terrific! Events that seemed so terrible in the end contained blessing.

If you look around, you will find Hashem's blessings everywhere. Let us be inspired to recognize and appreciate the blessings and abundance of Hashem's creations, as we say in *borei nefashos*: "He created many creatures and all that they need and many extras..."

Everything Hashem does is for good.

(*Berachos* 60b)

The more you look for Hashem's blessings, the more you will find!

Chapter 21

START YOUR DAY
WITH PRAYER

There is no better way to start your day than with praise to Hashem for all the blessings He bestows on us. Prayer helps us to think about all the good that He does and to thank Him for it. It opens our eyes to see the blessings.

> *The servant of G-d woke early and he went out, and behold an army had surrounded the city with horses and chariots. His servant said to him, "Master, what should we do?" Elisha answered, "Do not be afraid. We have more forces with us than they have with them!" Elisha then prayed and said, "Please open his eyes so that he may see..."*
>
> (*Melachim* II 6:15–17)

When Hashem opened the servant's eyes, the servant saw that he and Elisha were surrounded with an army of their own — an army of angels and a chariot of fire.

Often we don't see the blessings that surround us. When we pray to Hashem, we are opening our eyes to the good in this world that Hashem provides for us. Even more, when we appreciate the blessings Hashem gives us and pray with this intention, Hashem will answer our requests and bestow even more good upon us.

Every morning we recite fifteen blessings in which we thank Hashem for various gifts that He gives us, such as our ability to see. The fifteen blessings themselves contain a program for growth, each one building on the one before it. In order to sharpen our eyesight and focus on counting our blessings, it is worthwhile to study the fifteen daily morning blessings so that we can truly thank Hashem with heartfelt gratitude.

Count Your Blessings

"Count your blessings" is actually a Torah concept. The Rambam (*Hilchos Tefillah* 7:14) tells us that we should try to recite at least 100 blessings every day.

Chapter 22

A DISCERNING MIND

אשר נתן לשכוי בינה להבחין בין יום ובין לילה — *Thank you, Hashem, for giving the rooster the ability to understand the difference between day and night.*

In the first of the fifteen morning *berachos*, we thank Hashem for giving the rooster the ability to understand the difference between day and night. The word *sechvi* can be referring to a rooster, or it can be referring to the mind. Hashem provided people with the brains and insight to invent mechanical alarm clocks to help people wake up on time and serve Hashem at the beginning of every new day.

This quality of *bechinah*, the ability to make distinctions, such as distinguishing between night and day, is a major fundamental quality that is the foundation of *avodas Hashem* (see *Chovos HaLevavos, Sha'ar HaBechinah*).

The transition between day and night was created by Hashem in order to arouse us to be eager to grow and to utilize our daytime hours in the best way: to serve Him and perform mitzvos. If it would always be daytime, we would take it for granted. Hashem made the days change every twelve hours, from dark to light and back again, to arouse us to the recognition that He is in control.

Therefore, this *berachah* is the first of the fifteen blessings. Before we can even thank Hashem, we need to recognize that He is the one running the world and that all of the gifts for which we are grateful come from Him.

The Hidden Key

Although scientists have spent centuries studying the weather, the key to the weather is still in Hashem's hands. When it rains, sending us life-giving water, or the sun comes out, we know that these gifts have one Source: HaKadosh Baruch Hu!

Chapter 23

WHO AM I?

שלא עשני גוי — *Thank You, Hashem, for not creating me a non-Jew.*

The next few blessings are an expression of appreciation for the role Hashem created just for us. In the second blessing, we thank Hashem for giving us our Jewish identity.

This *berachah* comes right after the first *berachah* to teach us that if all people were the same and everyone had to fulfill 613 commandments, we would take it for granted just as if it were always daylight. A Jew is obligated to thank Hashem daily for the great privilege of having 613 mitzvos with which to elevate themselves and exalt and connect to the Creator of the universe.

If you had a choice between living in a beautiful mansion with seven rooms or a magnificent palace with 613 rooms, which would you choose?

Let us appreciate the gift of the mitzvos that we have been granted and the opportunity to reach the highest levels!

Chapter 24

TIME TO SERVE

שלא עשני עבד — *Thank You, Hashem, for not making me a slave.*

The next step, after we start thinking about our identity as Jews, is to focus on the practical: do we have the freedom to function as servants of Hashem?

We have been granted the greatest of gifts: the opportunity to serve the Creator and Controller of the universe. We are His servants, not servants of other servants!

The Talmud (*Chagigah* 9b) teaches that to qualify as an *eved Hashem*, a servant of Hashem, we need to learn our lessons 101 times. From this we learn the concept of striving for excellence.

This is the key to true success in life — to know and to apply ourselves to serving Hashem as a servant would serve his master, with complete dedication. Hashem is our ultimate boss and we can train ourselves to fulfill His instructions properly with joy.

One way to express our devotion is by focusing 100 percent on one mitzvah at a time to learn how to do it right. We can practice, for example, to say amen with sincere concentration and in this way perfect this mitzvah.

A true servant does his job well. Quality work, attention to detail, integrity, follow-up, and joy are some of the ingredients that are the hallmarks of a true dedicated servant. Let us apply these qualities in our service of Hashem, and we will be true *avdei Hashem*!

Chapter 25

THE FOUNDATION OF A JEWISH HOME

A man says:

שלא עשני אשה — *Thank You, Hashem, for not making me a woman.*

A woman says:

שעשני כרצונו — *Thank You, Hashem, for making me as You desired.*

A man and his wife are team members who work together to build a home to serve Hashem. In a team, each member has a specific role. In order for the team to be effective, each member knows his role and works together toward a common goal. Men and women were created to fill specific functions. After we thank Hashem for our Jewish identity and the freedom to serve Him, we thank Him for granting us our specific roles.

Rabbi Akiva's wife, Rachel, was the creative genius who motivated him to become great. He was the genius producer who followed the pathway to greatness by secluding himself in a yeshivah for twenty-four years. Each one had qualities that complemented the other and helped each other fulfill their potential.

Every morning when we recite the blessings, we thank Hashem for giving us our specific role with which to serve Him. A man thanks Hashem, for example, for his ongoing obligation to study Torah, whereas a woman thanks Hashem for her ability to have and raise children.

Build a Jewish Home

Rav Avigdor Miller, zt"l, taught (*Awake My Glory*, p. 338) the three fundamental ideals of a Jewish home:

1. to establish a home that is like a mini Beis HaMikdash, in which the goal and desire is to serve Hashem;

2. to raise a generation of children to serve Hashem;

3. to serve as an opportunity to do *chesed* — to show kindness to one another by thinking of the other, and not only of oneself.

Chapter 26
OPEN YOUR EYES

פוקח עורים — *Thank You, Hashem, for opening the eyes of the blind.*

Now that we know who we are and appreciate our role in life, we thank Hashem for providing us our basic needs with which to serve Him. First, we thank Him for granting us eyesight.

When we analyze the formulation of the blessing, we notice something strange. We are thanking Hashem for "opening the eyes of the 'blind.' " In other words, our eyes were closed, and when we awoke and opened them, we were able to see. For this, we thank Hashem.

Why did Hashem create us with eyes that have covers (i.e., eyelids) which close when we are tired and then open when we are refreshed?

One benefit of the eyelids is that they serve as reminders that we should appreciate the great gift that is our eyes. To illustrate, if you are sitting in a quiet place, you can try the following experiment:

Close your eyes for one minute and think: I cannot read a page of this book with my eyes closed.

Now open your eyes and say, "Wow, what a gift! Hashem is now giving me the power to open my eyes and decipher the markings on this page by sending the information to my brain for instant processing!"

The eyes not only show you the image that is in front of them, but they "take" automatic photos constantly and send these images to the brain, which processes the information it receives in miraculous ways. Not only does Hashem open our eyes to see, but in essence He also opens our mind to process what we are seeing. By giving us the ability to close our eyes and open them, we can appreciate this gift so much more.

> It is interesting to note that the Sefaradi version of the prayers contains a different order of *berachos*. There the second blessing is "Hashem opens up our eyes." They go directly to appreciating the eyes before going on to the other blessings.

Chapter 27
APPRECIATE YOUR CLOTHING

מלביש ערומים — *Thank You, Hashem, for clothing the naked.*

How can it be? After thanking Hashem for the wondrous gift of eyesight, we thank Him for...clothing? Why does the blessing for clothing follow our blessing for the grand miracle of eyesight?

One lesson we learn here is that we need to be grateful for every detail of the gifts we receive daily, whether it is something as miraculous as eyesight or something less sensational like clothing. The more we are thankful to Hashem, the more we enjoy the benefits we receive and the more we will receive.

The word for "clothing," *malbush* (מלבוש), comes from the words *lo bushah* (לא בושה), without shame. Clothing covers the shame of a person and protects his dignity. Our clothing highlights the idea that the body is not the essential "I" — it is only a cover for the *neshamah*, the soul which is the core of who we are.

The wording of this *berachah* presents a contrast — the clothed versus the unclothed. We are reminded here of those who suffer from a lack of clothing and we are grateful that we are so blessed.

Clothing limits our eyesight by covering that which should not be seen. Thus we thank Hashem for
1. eyes to see and
2. clothing to cover what should not be seen.

Chapter 28
SIT UP!

מתיר אסורים — *Thank You, Hashem, for releasing those who are bound.*

This blessing is an expression of gratitude to Hashem for giving us the ability to get up in the morning — to sit up in our beds and prepare to start our day (*Berachos* 60b).

Why does the blessing for sitting up use such strange wording? What does *"matir assurim,"* releasing the bound, have to do with sitting up?

This blessing helps us focus on why we are getting up in the morning:

A tzaddik may fall seven times, but he keeps getting up.

(*Mishlei* 24:16)

Sitting up is symbolic of improving ourselves to achieve higher levels in life. We all need a boost to change and improve our ways. We need to sit up and take notice of the fact that we need to improve. A little bit of growth, which starts with sitting up in the morning and preparing to start the day right, is a great accomplishment.

Not only do we thank Hashem for the ability to symbolically sit up — for being able to start the day anew and make changes — but we also thank Him for the ability to physically sit up. With this *berachah*, we are saying, "Thank You, Hashem, for enabling Me to move my limbs, to push myself up and remain balanced in a sitting position." This in itself is amazing!

We should not take sitting for granted. Every morning we should try to focus on developing a feeling of gratitude to thank Hashem sincerely for this precious gift.

If you see someone who cannot move without assistance, you pray that they should get well, and you also learn to say this blessing with more joy!

Chapter 29

RISING TO THE OCCASION

זוקף כפופים — *Thank You, Hashem, for keeping upright those who were bent.*

Like the previous blessing, we are not only thanking Hashem for our ability to physically stand up. This blessing also expresses thanks for being able to move on to another stage of development, which represents an even higher level.

There are five basic benefits that we gain from being able to balance ourselves with an upright posture:

❖ We have a better view of our surroundings from a higher perch.

❖ A straight position is more comfortable.

❖ It gives us more dignity.

❖ It makes us feel closer to Heaven, the place where

Hashem's glory resides.

❖ It enables us to fulfill the great mitzvah to bow down in Hashem's honor at the appropriate places in our prayers.

When we say this blessing, we are thanking Hashem for both the physical and the spiritual benefits of this daily miracle.

Wake-Up Call

Every morning, when we get out of bed and stand upright, we are reminded to think of the opportunity we have to make the most of the new day. Let us take advantage of this daily opportunity while we are still alive and able to function.

Chapter 30

SOLID GROUND

רוקע הארץ על המים — *Thank You, Hashem, for spreading out the earth upon the waters.*

A fter we thank Hashem for the ability to stand upright, we thank Him for giving us something to stand on. Hashem constantly keeps the earth positioned right where we need it when we stand up.

When we sit, stand, walk, or lay down, we are being supported by Hashem's earth. When we hear about a pool of quicksand or a sudden sinkhole that causes untold damages and harm, *chas v'shalom*, we are alerted to how grateful we should be when the earth remains a solid support for us.

World of Water
Look at a globe. You will observe that most of the world is made up of water, and the land masses rest on top of it. Yet the continents and islands do not sink into the water because Hashem keeps them in place!

Chapter 31

ALL MY NEEDS

שעשה לי כל צרכי — *Thank You, Hashem, for supplying me with all of my needs.*

Hashem has provided us with the tools we need to accomplish in this world: eyesight, assistance in achieving higher levels, the ground on which we stand... Now we thank Hashem for giving us our specific mission in life.

This is the only *berachah* of these fifteen morning *berachos* where we specify our individuality, as it says, *"she'asah li* — for supplying *me...*"* This blessing implies that each of us are provided with our specific needs in mind to accomplish our individual mission. Here we are reminded that each of us has a unique portion for which we should be thankful.

Every person is obligated to say:

The world was created because of me!

(*Sanhedrin* 37a)

We need to develop the incredible perspective of looking at the whole world with this vision: it is for my benefit! With this idea in our minds, we will have the confidence to fulfill our mission, because we are the only ones who can.

Rose-Colored Glasses
What kind of "glasses" are you wearing?
Are you viewing the world through Torah lenses — through a Torah and mitzvah perspective?
Or, are you using glasses you don't even realize are there, coloring your vision?

Chapter 32

FOOTSTEPS

המכין מצעדי גבר — *Thank You, Hashem, for preparing the footsteps of a person.*

Now that we recognize our mission, we can ask ourselves, "Where should I go now? What do I need to do today to develop my potential?" On this, the Mishnah gives us guidance:

The world stands on three pillars: Torah study, prayer, and kindness.

(*Avos* 1:2)

Let us ask ourselves: What should I learn, what should I pray for, and whom should I help? When we apply these questions to our unique mission, we will know exactly which direction to take.

This blessing uses the term *hameichin*, "prepare." This is the key to this *berachah*. The work of achieving the goals that are defined by our position in life requires *hachanah*, preparation and planning. Hashem "prepares a person's footsteps" — He sets things up for us to learn the lessons we need to know. Thus, each footstep we take in our own unique path leads us to the opportunities and challenges that we are supposed to face in order to succeed in life.

> The secret to success is to take small steps to advance our goals — one small step at a time, with Hashem's help, will take us to where we are supposed to be.

Chapter 33

FEEL THE POWER

אוזר ישראל בגבורה — *Thank You, Hashem, for girding Jews with strength.*

What is the source of our strength? Our power comes in many forms:

Who is wise? One who sees the potential one can gain when one learns from others.

Who is strong? One who sees the need to conquer and control his own inclination.

Who is wealthy? One who focuses on appreciating and rejoicing with all of the portions Hashem has provided for him.

Who is honorable? One who sees that others deserve honor.

(Based on *Avos* 4:1)

Feel the Power

The four qualities that the *mishnah* enumerates give us our power and strength. They are the traits we need to become a complete person. Here are some ways that these traits help us develop into who we need to become:

1. Learn from others and realize that they are agents from Hashem.

2. See that real strength comes from conquering your inclinations.

3. Realize how much abundance Hashem supplies you with and appreciate your unique portion.

4. Honor others and you will receive honor in turn.

Hashem provides us with the opportunity to develop our talents, to improve our character traits, and to shine with the gifts we have to offer the world. All we need to do is take it.

Chapter 34

SEE THE GLORY

עוטר ישראל בתפארה — *Thank You, Hashem, for crowning Jews with glory.*

"Crowns of glory" refers to our head coverings, which remind a person to be aware of Hashem above us. It also refers to the tefillin men wear on their heads during prayer.

We already said a blessing for clothing. Why is there a separate blessing for a head covering? And why is this considered a person's glory?

The Talmud says a strong statement regarding head coverings:

Cover your head so that you will attain a fear of Heaven.

(*Shabbos* 156b)

Our head coverings remind us that Hashem, who created us and cares for us, has given us a Torah to follow, which teaches us how to fulfill our purpose in this world. Having a special blessing on head coverings highlights and emphasizes this idea.

> The secret of the giving of the Torah is to teach the awareness that Hashem is the absolute G-d; there is no other besides Him.
>
> (*Da'as Torah*, p. 140)

Chapter 35

FEEL THE STRENGTH

הנותן ליעף כח — *Thank You, Hashem, for giving strength to the tired.*

Hashem invented sleep so that we could take a break from our activities. Ideally we should rest about eight hours, a third of the twenty-four-hour day (Rambam, *Hilchos De'os* 4:4). This gives us the energy we need to be active and do our work in the daytime.

Hashem could have invented a system where we need only ten-minute intervals of sleep rather than eight hours each night. Why did He choose this method?

Our Sages teach us that one of the reasons for this is to remind us of our need for Him to reenergize us every night — not only to supply physical energy, but spiritual energy as well. When we wake up after eight hours of sleep, we are so thankful to Hashem for waking us up. This infuses us with *emunah* and *bitachon* that will help us jumpstart a day filled with *avodas Hashem*.

A ten-minute sleeping pill will not have the same effect. It takes our need for sleep to change us so that we trust in Hashem's provisions and recognize and appreciate the abundant blessings that we receive from Him.

> A nap is also a gift from Hashem. An afternoon nap can make one feel like a new person, refreshed and ready to face the rest of the day. Let us thank Him for this precious gift!

Chapter 36

FULL VISION

המעביר שינה מעיני ותנומה מעפעפי — *Thank You, Hashem, for removing sleep from my eyes and slumber from my eyelids.*

In this blessing, it seems that we are thanking Hashem for two things that we already thanked Him for: for waking us up and for allowing us to open our eyes. Why did the Sages institute another blessing for these gifts?

With this *berachah* we express our thanks, not only for opening our eyes and waking us up, but for waking us up refreshed and alert. The Talmud explains (*Berachos* 60b) that one says this blessing after washing one's face, which brings him to wake up fully.

Our Sages are teaching us that we need Hashem's help at each step of the way. The time between waking up and full awareness is small, but even for this we need to thank Hashem, because we could not make this small step without His help. Every step in life can make a great difference in how we develop. We need Hashem's help to steer us in the right direction.

This blessing is the beginning of a long blessing that asks Hashem for what we need for a proper start to a successful day. In this lengthy *berachah*, we request of Him: "Hashem, please assist us in connecting with Your Torah, clinging to Your mitzvos, and avoiding the negative." We elaborate on these ideas because they are so essential to our *avodas Hashem*.

This last *berachah* is long for a good reason: it needs to encompass everything we need to face our day. It emphasizes that when we are provided with the right tools and environment, we can truly grow and put all of the energy Hashem has infused us with upon waking to good use. We can transform ourselves from someone who is uncertain about which direction he is headed to a person who knows exactly what he needs to do in order to achieve great levels of perfection.

There is nothing more important in life than Torah study, serving Hashem with prayer, and helping other people. We pray to Hashem to set up our environment so that it will be conducive to serving Him properly.

Six Constant Mitzvos

Connect with and serve Hashem with the six mitzvos that apply all the time, every day:

1. To be aware of Hashem
2. To believe there is no other besides Him
3. To believe that He is One
4. To love Him
5. To fear Him
6. Not to stray away from Him

GUARDING AGAINST THE EVIL EYE

Chapter 37

THE POWER OF THE EYES

The Gra explains that seeing is more powerful than hearing (*Biur HaGra, Tikunei Zohar* 40). He gives some examples of how seeing is greater:

❖ One can see a greater distance than one can hear.

❖ One can see more in one minute than it would take to hear the same amount of information in a longer period of time.

❖ One remembers what one saw for a longer period of time than one remembers what one heard.

Since the sense of sight is more powerful than the sense of hearing, it makes a stronger impression and thus has a greater power to influence us. Therefore, the Torah tells us:

Do not follow after your heart and after your eyes.
(Bemidbar 15:39)

The secret to avoiding sin is to guard your eyes. Closing one's eyes from seeing evil can save a person from committing the worst of sins, such as

- ❖ *idolatry* — by avoiding even gazing at such abominations;

- ❖ *immorality* — by avoiding gazing at women one may not marry;

- ❖ *murder* — by avoiding gazing at wicked people.

Focusing one's eyes on Torah study, prayers, and positive sights, on the other hand, will enable and empower a person to live properly and to grow in serving Hashem.

Rabbi Yehoshua said: "An evil eye, the evil inclination, and hatred of others remove a person from the world."

(*Avos* 2:11)

Chapter 38

RESISTING TEMPTATION

In the previous chapter, we mentioned that the sense of sight is so powerful that it can influence a person to sin. Indeed, the Torah teaches us that the path to resisting temptation is by learning not to follow after everything our eyes see, as we are taught:

> "Do not stray after your heart and after your eyes" (Bemidbar 15:39) — the eye sees, the heart desires, and the body commits the sin.
>
> (Rashi, quoting Midrash Tanchuma)

This is what caused the first sin in history, as the Torah testifies:

> She saw that it was good to eat and it was appealing to the eyes and she ate...
>
> (Bereishis 3:6)

How do we prevent ourselves from following after our eyes and giving in to temptation?

Mesilas Yesharim (15) teaches that we need to consider the negative aspects of indulging, both the immediate and long-term effects. We have to train ourselves to recognize the fallacies of indulging in what our eyes see. We must ask ourselves: It may look good, but is it really good for us?

It is like being on a diet and you are tempted by a delicious-looking chocolate cake. How can you resist taking a bite? Ask yourself:

How long will the pleasure from eating the cake last? Is it really worth breaking my healthy diet for a few moments of enjoyment?

What will the effects be — harmful or beneficial? Consider the many illnesses that can come from eating unhealthy foods. Do you really want to indulge in a fleeting pleasure when it means that you will suffer later?

What about the more immediate effects? Consider the heaviness, discomfort, and sluggishness that sets in after eating unhealthy, fatty foods.

Consider the benefits of the alternative: You can be just as full from healthy foods, which won't harm you. On the contrary, they are beneficial to your body.

In this way, you can learn how to resist temptation and focus on the correct path.

Optical Illusions

When faced with temptation, remember: you can choose. Why follow the optical illusions of temptation when you can reap the enduring benefits of following the way of the Torah?

Chapter 39

OPEN AND SHUT

After relating the sin of Adam and Chavah, the To-rah says something strange:

Their eyes were opened and they realized that they were undressed.

(Bereishis 3:7)

What does this mean? Adam and Chavah's eyes had been open all along!

It means that now they became aware of that which they had ignored previously. After their sin, they began noticing the wrong things. The physical became a concern. (Of course, we don't truly understand what this means, since Adam and Chavah were so much greater than us. But we can learn lessons as they apply on our level.) When a person focuses on trivial, unnecessary matters, he begins to be lured by temptations and thereby requires more of an effort to choose between right and wrong.

Every morning we thank Hashem for "opening the eyes of the blind" — for providing us with the ability to see. Immediately after, we thank Him for supplying us with clothing. Why are these two blessings next to each other?

We are obligated to wear clothing to cover the parts of the body that may lead us to see things in the wrong perspective. The eyes can still see, but the clothing serves to block the eyes from seeing what it shouldn't. This teaches us that we have to learn to focus on what Hashem wants us to see in our lives:

See that...

❖ you have incredible reserves of strength, character, and resilience;

❖ new doors will keep opening for you in life — Hashem keeps sending you opportunities for growth;

❖ hardships are only temporary setbacks that can lead you to greater spiritual levels;

❖ Hashem gave you *bechirah*, free will, to decide what to do with the situations Hashem sends you.

The eye resembles a miniature world. The white area surrounding the pupil is like the oceans surrounding land; the round center resembles the sun... Why does this part of the body resemble the world? Because the way we see things makes all the difference for everything in life!

(Based on *Bechoros* 16a, *Rashi*)

Chapter 40

THE EVIL EYE

Ninety-nine [out of a hundred] people pass away due to an evil eye, and one due to other causes.

(*Bava Metzia* 107b)

We are told that when one praises someone's wealth, wisdom, children, etc., one should always say, *"Bli ayin hara* — without an evil eye" (*Minchas Eliezer* 6:6). One who "eyes" someone else's good fortune, or who behaves in an ostentatious manner, may cause ill feelings. This may evoke a heavenly judgment, causing the heavenly tribunal to examine the person's "rights" to that good fortune. When the person is put under heavenly scrutiny, he may be judged as lacking merit and lose the good that he has.

Thus, it is important to always be sensitive to people's feelings. If you were granted a fortune, don't flaunt it. If you were blessed with many children, be sensitive to those who are not so fortunate. Similarly, one who receives a blessing from a Torah sage for some special need should keep the matter a secret as much as possible. If it becomes publicized prematurely, it may not come to fruition, due to an evil eye (*Divrei Torah* 2:53).

On the other hand, if you see someone who has good fortune, try to view that person with a good eye and be happy for him. Appreciate the fact that Hashem gives everyone exactly what he needs and there is no need to feel envy for someone else's "portion."

Who is truly wealthy? One who rejoices with "his" portion!

(*Avos* 4:1)

Chapter 41
SOUL BLEMISHES

The Torah lists three types of eye problems that can disqualify a *kohen* from serving in the Beis HaMikdash:

> *If his brows are abnormally long, or if he has a cataract, or a dry skin eruption in his eye...*

(*Vayikra* 21:20)

The Gemara (*Megillah* 28a) explains that the word *gibein*, "long eyebrows," hints at the reason why the mountains of the world were rejected from serving as the site for receiving the Torah. Long eyebrows are symbolic of arrogance (the word *gibein* has the same root as *gavohah*, high), which can disqualify a person from becoming close to Hashem. Hashem chose Sinai because of its humble posture. The Gemara concludes: "One who is arrogant is a blemished person."

In one sense, when you see yourself, you are looking at the most important person in the world, as it says, "Every person is obligated to say: The world was created because of me!" (*Sanhedrin* 37a). At the same time we have to remember: "A person is but dust and ashes" (based on *Bereishis* 18:27). This humbles us and reminds us that compared to Hashem, we are like dust and we exist only because of Hashem's beneficence.

We need a balance of both of these views to be able to accomplish our mission in life. Sometimes we need a boost and we need to remind ourselves that we are the only ones who can accomplish our specific purpose. On the other hand, we need to remember that we are only human — we need to be grateful to Hashem who gave us life and sustains us, and we need to prepare for the Day of Judgment before Hashem, to whom we have to account for our deeds. By keeping the danger of arrogance in check, we will surely thrive and come closer to Hashem.

The sense of sight is powerful, indeed. Not only the sights you see in the outside world, but also how you envision yourself affect your actions and may influence you to sin or to do good. How you use the power of your eyes is up to you.

Every day we say in our prayers: והאר עינינו בתורתך — "Please, Hashem, illuminate our eyes with the magnificent light of the Torah so that our hearts and minds may cling to Your mitzvos, to love and fear You..." (*Ahavah Rabbah*, the morning blessing before the Shema).

SAGE VISION

Chapter 42

LOOKING FOR ANSWERS

*Rabbi Yehoshua ben Perachyah says: Establish for
yourself a teacher...*

(Avos 1:6)

A *rav* or a *talmid chacham* who has a great knowledge
of Torah sees the world differently from other
people. His view of the world comes through "Torah
lenses." With their superior Torah knowledge, sages
are generally not fooled by the appearance of things —
they see through the superficial and can define their
true value. That is why it is so important to establish
for yourself a *rav* — because he will bring a vision of
the world into your life that otherwise you would not
have.

Everyone faces situations in life where it is hard to
see the right path. The choices may look equally right
or equally wrong. How can you know which road to

take? That is why you go to a *rav*, a Torah sage, who, with his Torah knowledge, can see the road clearly.

Some people think that they should not bother a *rav* with their questions. Or they think that they should not be having any questions at all. It is okay to have questions — as long as you are searching for answers. One way to find those answers is by asking someone greater and more knowledgeable than you. Why learn the hard way and make mistakes when you can connect with a mentor and get it right the first time?

At certain times, where the Sages put their eyes the results were death or poverty.

(*Mo'ed Katan* 17b)

The Sages' sight was so powerful that they could bring a punishment upon a person who was deserving of it. In most cases, the positive is even more powerful than the negative — if the Sages could bring misfortune to those who deserved it, imagine the effects of their beneficial blessings! With their Torah vision, they could bring blessings to those who needed it.

In the next few chapters we will study the "sage vision" of our Sages to learn and benefit from their words of wisdom.

Questions for Thought

Who was the greatest teacher you have ever known?

How did you benefit from his influence?

What did you learn from his teaching style?

A good teacher can change your life forever — if you will let him.

Chapter 43

RABBI ZAKKAI: PRAYER AND RESPECT

The Sages could see through the superficial issues of life and penetrate to the truth with the Torah's guidance. They left us with a body of knowledge — the Mishnah and Talmud — in which they passed down Hashem's wisdom. Through their lessons, we too can learn to see the truth.

One Talmudic discussion (*Megillah* 27b) that gives us a wealth of knowledge is about how a person can earn the merits that will bring him a long life. Four Sages were interviewed and asked: "What did you do to merit longevity?" Each Sage gave a three-part answer. Rabbi Zakkai said:

1. He was always careful to maintain the cleanliness of his place for prayer.

2. He never called people by nicknames.

3. He was always careful to honor Shabbos.

All of these areas in which Rabbi Zakkai was careful involve some aspect of respect or honor.

Rabbi Zakkai was careful to care for his specific place of prayer. He showed honor to Hashem and respect for the mitzvah of prayer by ensuring that he would have an appropriate place to daven. His particular care in this mitzvah surely affected his prayers and made them more effective. One of the main things we ask for in our prayers, in one form or another, is longevity so that we can serve Hashem better. Surely it was his powerful prayers that resulted in his meriting a long life.

When we honor others, we help them live longer. People who are treated with respect have greater peace of mind and are better able to succeed. This surely improves their quality of life and makes them live longer. Thus, measure for measure, we too deserve a long life. Rabbi Zakkai showed respect for others by calling them by their proper names. In this merit, he earned the reward of longevity.

Finally, by honoring Shabbos we pay tribute to the Creator of all life. This is manifest when we say Kiddush, in which we proclaim that Hashem, the Creator of life, rested on Shabbos. Since Hashem rested, we stop and rest in order to focus on our relationship with Hashem.

This is the lesson of Rabbi Zakkai: If we devote our lives to serving Hashem with prayer, respecting others, and honoring and celebrating His special day every week, we will merit the great reward of a long life.

Friday Night Blessings

We can fulfill all three of Rabbi Zakkai's principles every Friday night, when we bless our children:

1. Include a prayer that they should live long healthy lives.
2. Call them by their proper names.
3. Honor the Shabbos by teaching them that when we celebrate Shabbos properly, Hashem will bless us with His great blessings.

Chapter 44

RABBI ELAZAR BEN SHAMUA: KINDNESS AND BLESSINGS

The second Sage who was interviewed was Rabbi Elazar ben Shamua. He answered with a three-part formula of his own:

1. He never took a shortcut through a shul.

2. He never "stepped on" the heads of holy people.

3. He always blessed Jews with the appropriate blessings.

Prayer is an ongoing daily requirement to request and plead to the Master of life to extend our time here. But to pray properly, we need to respect the setting of our prayers. A shul is a holy place, where we can communicate with Hashem more easily than anywhere else. How can one walk through a shul just to get to the other side? That is why Rabbi Elazar was always careful never to use a shul simply as a shortcut.

Second, the way we treat others, the way we interact with them, causes Hashem to deal with us in like manner. Every person we honor, in all types of situations, can have an effect on our lives. Rabbi Zakkai was careful to call people by their proper names; Rabbi Elazar showed respect by honoring those who had earned it.

Finally, the way we bless each other influences the blessings that Hashem bestows on us. When we pray that Hashem should prolong the lives of our fellow Jews, we ourselves merit this blessing.

You Shall Be Blessed

The Gemara (*Megillah* 27b) teaches that it is always important to respond to a blessing with the words, וכן למר — "You should also be blessed the same way." Today, many respond with the Hebrew words "*Gam atem* — You also [should be so blessed]" or "*Baruch tiheyeh* — You should be blessed," to convey the same idea.

Chapter 45

RABBI PREIDAH: TORAH AND HONOR

The third Sage who was asked, "What did you do to merit long life?" was Rabbi Preidah. This Sage is famous from the episode mentioned in *Eiruvin* (54b), in which a heavenly voice proclaimed that he would live 400 years because he taught a disciple every lesson 400 times. Surprisingly, this quality is not mentioned as one of his three answers. Rather, he said:

1. He was always first in the *beis midrash*.

2. He would never lead the *bentching* if there was a *kohen* present.

3. He never ate meat from an animal if *kohanim* did not receive their portions of that animal first.

Why are we in this world and how can we prolong our stay? The obvious answer is that if we focus on why we are here, we can justify an extension. Rabbi

Preidah lived four hundred years. Why? It starts with the fact that he never came late to the study hall! His intense focus was on our primary purpose in life: to study Hashem's Torah.

But there is a concern: if someone lives four hundred years, how will he get along with people younger than him, who are fifty, sixty, or seventy years old, the ones who are usually the honored elders?

Thus Rabbi Preidah followed with steps 2 and 3, showing that he was very careful to always accord everyone with the honor and respect they deserved.

Still, we are left with the question: Why didn't Rabbi Preidah mention the secret of teaching a disciple four hundred times? Isn't this what brought him longevity, as the heavenly voice proclaimed? *Tosafos* asks this question and gives two answers, one of which is "This and that were the cause." What does this mean?

If we examine Rabbi Preidah's three-step formula, we see that they are based on two general principles that encompass all of life: (1) he always utilized his Torah study time to the maximum, and (2) he was sensitive to other people's needs to the point that he devoted a huge amount of time to teaching others according to their specific requirements.

Rabbi Preidah didn't mention his remarkable act of teaching his disciple four hundred times when asked why he merited longevity. That was just one isolated case among many, illustrating how he followed his principles to their fullest limits and beyond.

Time Well Spent

Doing something 400 times takes time, but that is the gift of life — that we can devote time to Hashem's causes and He compensates us, measure for measure.

Chapter 46

RABBI NECHUNYAH BEN HAKANAH: FORMS OF KINDNESS

The fourth Sage who was asked how he had merited longevity gave three qualities of kindness in his list:

1. He never derived honor from someone else's shame.

2. He would make peace with everyone before going to sleep every night.

3. He was always generous with his money and made sure to give each person who asked something extra.

Here are three aspects of *chesed*, kindness, that one can do for others: showing honor, making peace, and providing their financial needs. These are all areas that improve a person's quality of life. When we try to improve the quality of life of others, then, measure for measure, Hashem will give us long life. Thus, Rabbi Nechunyah, who excelled in these three areas, merited longevity.

Looking in Two Directions

Why did Hashem give us two eyes? One of the great lessons we learn is that we have to always (1) *look* to fulfill our obligations toward Hashem and (2) also *see* the needs of others.

Chapter 47

RABBI YEHOSHUA BEN KARCHA: VISION TO LONGEVITY

R abbi Yehoshua ben Karcha was also asked this question: "What did you do to merit a long life?" His answer was different from the other four Sages. Rather than give a list of the good acts that he performed, he answered: "I never gazed at the form of a wicked person" (*Megillah* 28a).

The Gemara asks: Why is this a merit for longevity? It is known that one who gazes at wicked people develops a deficiency in his eyesight, as Yitzchak Avinu suffered from gazing at his son Esav. Furthermore, Rav Akiva Eiger writes that just to look is permissible, but to gaze intently, to think about the face and form of a wicked person, is harmful. Why did Rabbi Yehoshua ben Karcha receive a reward for something that no one should do because it is harmful?

Rabbi Yehoshua ben Karcha realized that we are influenced by what we see. Everything he did, even where he focused his eyes, was solely for the purpose of serving Hashem. Because he excelled in this principle of not gazing at the wicked, he merited longevity.

Life Is for Living

Your eyes should see your teacher.

(*Yeshayahu* 30:20)

Every person has something to teach us ("Who is wise? One who learns from every person" — *Avos* 4:1). But if a person chooses to oppose eternal values, it is dangerous to turn to him for lessons. It is wise not to even look at him, because the effects of his influence can be harmful.

Chapter 48

RABBI AKIVA: STRIVING TO EXCEL

When Rabbi Akiva was young, he asked Rabbi Nechunya HaGadol (not to be confused with Rabbi Nechunyah HaKanah): "What is your secret to longevity?"

Rabbi Akiva was still unknown at that time, and Rabbi Nechunya's servants thought he was being disrespectful, so they chased him up a tree. He called down, "I have a question: Why does it say, 'One sheep is to be brought daily in the morning'?" ("A sheep" would suffice — it would be obvious that it is only one.)

When Rabbi Nechunya heard Rabbi Akiva's question, the older Sage saw that here was a young Torah scholar. He told his servants, "Leave him alone. The answer to his question is: 'One' means take the most unique, the best animal for a *korban*."

Why was this the point that Rabbi Akiva chose to ask about in order to gain the attention of Rabbi Nechunya?

This was a clue to what he was asking when he asked for Rabbi Nechunya's secret to longevity. He was hinting, "I know that Hashem wants us to bring our best animal as an offering. And if we do our best for Hashem, I assume that Hashem then enables us to live longer in return. Give me some guidelines as to how I can excel in life."

Rabbi Nechunya answered with three tips:

1. Don't accept gifts.

2. Don't be stubborn.

3. Be generous.

Hashem gave each person unique abilities, talents, and sensibilities. But people tend to become beholden to others, which limits their free will to choose what is best for themselves as individuals. Thus, *Mishlei* (15:27) teaches: "Those who hate gifts will live."

Life is defined by how much free will a person utilizes to make the right choices. One who refuses to accept gifts, thus utilizing his free will to live a better life as an individual who serves Hashem in his unique way, deserves more life as a gift from Hashem, measure for measure.

But this might lead to a tendency to always want things your way, which may lead to hurting others. Thus, part 2 of the formula is to always be flexible and to cooperate with others, and part 3 of this equation is to be more generous, giving of yourself to help others enjoy life more.

All of the Sages' answers to the question "What did you do to merit longevity?" share similar aspects: they all involve areas of respect and kindness, whether showing honor to Hashem by being careful in prayer and honoring Shabbos or respecting others. Yet each was different; each had his own path.

Train each youth according to his way.

(*Mishlei* 22:5)

There are different pathways in which a person can excel, based on the nature of each person's personality. When a person looks for a *rav* to be his mentor and guide, he must find someone who will advise him "according to his way." The *rav* must recognize the person's individual path and guide him to make the right choices according to his personality and character traits.

That is also why one cannot act according to an answer that a *rav* gave to one's friend. The *rav* gave his friend advice based on his unique situation and tendencies. If you were to ask the same *rav* the same question, you might receive a different answer. Thus, "establish for yourself a *rav*" — one who will guide you on your unique path.

The Mishnah in *Avos* 1:6 advises:

1. Make for yourself a teacher.
2. Acquire for yourself a friend.
3. Judge every person favorably.

What is the connection between the third instruction and the first two?

Step 3 teaches us that each person is an individual with his own thought patterns. With this in mind, we will be able to relate to a mentor and get along with our friends.

LOOK TO
HASHEM

Chapter 49

SEEING HASHEM IN OUR LIVES

Try closing one eye and looking straight ahead. Now open both eyes and see how much more you can see.

There are many different ways of looking at something. You can focus on the details and just see trees, or step back and see the whole forest. You can focus on the small details, or you can "lift up your eyes on high to see Who created these" (*Yeshayahu* 40:26). In this way, you look beyond the obvious to recognize the Master, Designer, Creator, and Controller of all.

The saying "Hashem is in the details" is certainly true. But Hashem is also in the big picture. In fact, He is in every part of the picture. All we need to do is step back and let ourselves see it.

I place Hashem before me always.

(*Tehillim* 17:8)

This *pasuk* teaches us the most fundamental truth of life: Hashem is the Source of everything in existence. But you can choose to close your eyes to this fact. You can choose to go about life believing that everything that happens is just a coincidence, an accident. In order to see Hashem in your life, you need to open your eyes, your mind, and your heart. You must "place Hashem before you always."

How can you reframe your "glasses" so that you will see that Hashem is behind everything that happens in this world?

The answer goes back to looking for Hashem in the big picture. If you focus on one person or one company or one event as the source of your good fortune — or misfortune — you are in trouble. You are just focusing on the details. Instead, step back and realize that they are merely agents of Hashem. It is not they who caused the misfortune; it came from Hashem and ultimately it is good for you — even if you don't see it yet! (You may have heard the joke about the man who was asked, "Do you believe in Hashem?" and he answered, "Well, someone is out to get me!")

He may be using one avenue now to send us blessings or challenges, but He has many other avenues at His disposal. When we understand that the true Source of all blessings — as well as the trials — is not people nor organizations nor even coincidence, but Hashem alone, then we are seeing Hashem in the big picture of our life. As we open our inner eyes, the eyes of our *neshamah*, we see more and more of Hashem's providence, how He cares for us and nurtures us.

When Moshe Rabbeinu asked Hashem, "Please show me Your glory" (*Shemos* 33:18), Hashem answered, "You shall see My back" (ibid. 33:23). The full meaning of these verses are beyond our comprehension, but we still learn many profound lessons from these passages. One lesson is that we can learn to see, to appreciate, and to recognize that Hashem is the Creator and Controller of everything by connecting the dots of past events.

We can "look back" at the big picture of our lives and see how masterful and magnificent are Hashem's ways.

Avraham's Famous Hospitality

Avraham Avinu was the first person to do *kiruv rechokim*. He and his wife, Sarah, would organize lavish banquets and invite people from near and far to enjoy his hospitality. At the end of the feast, as the Talmud teaches (*Sotah* 10b), the people would rise to thank Avraham.

That is when he would teach them about Hashem. He would explain that all of the food that they had just enjoyed had come from Hashem, who created the world, and it was He who needed to be thanked.

Avraham wasn't just giving them food to eat. He was giving them much more: he provided them with a learning experience to recognize and believe in Hashem, a chance that they, too, would see Hashem in their lives.

Chapter 50

TRUST IN HASHEM

Jump in and the sea will split!

This is what happened to the Jewish people when they faced the waters of the Red Sea. One man had the faith and courage to "take the plunge" — once Nachshon ben Aminadav jumped in, the sea split and the rest of the Jewish people followed.

In order to accomplish what we need to achieve in our life, we need to "take the plunge." We need to have the courage to believe and trust in Hashem.

How do we "take the plunge"? First, by recognizing that Hashem is in control. Hashem created every part of us; He sustains us and keeps the world running. We must do our part, and leave everything else to Him.

The tool that Hashem gave us to help us trust in Him is prayer. But we need to avoid telling Hashem how He should help us. We must accept that He knows better than anyone else how to make things right for us (even if we don't always see it!).

When we pray, we ask Hashem for our general needs and then let Hashem fill in the details. His resources are unlimited and His planning is perfect. We need only to focus on placing our trust in Hashem and let Him do the rest.

Open an opening the size of the eye of a needle, and Hashem will open for you an opening the size of a hall.

(Midrash, *Shir HaShirim*)

Sometimes, we try to "pry" a door open, but it seems stuck. The solution is to turn "pry" into "pray" — pray to Hashem sincerely, with your full concentration, and Hashem will answer your prayers. (In times of stress, it is recommended to say chapter 23 of *Tehillim* slowly, verse by verse, word by word.)

Chapter 51

LOVE HASHEM

A woman came to a *rav* with a dilemma. She said, "Two men have approached me and asked me to marry them. How should I decide which one to marry?"

The *rav* answered: "Neither of them. If you have to ask me to choose, it is clear that you don't feel enough of a connection with them and should not marry either one."

It is a mitzvah to love Hashem. It should be our goal to develop a solid connection with Him so that everything we do is for His sake. The choice will be clear; in everything we do, we will choose to serve Hashem, on whom we focus all of our devotion and love.

But how can a person be commanded to feel love? Is it really possible to develop a love for Hashem?

The Rambam teaches us that we can indeed develop this emotion. He says:

How does a person come to love and fear Hashem? When he contemplates Hashem's ways and His magnificent creations and He sees from them His profound, incredible wisdom, he will immediately respond with love, praise, admiration...

(Hilchos Yesodei HaTorah 2:2)

This is the secret to developing a love for Hashem: by appreciating all the wonderful good that He does for us.

Take an apple. Consider how Hashem designed this compact, colorful, magnificent, beautiful — and tasty — masterpiece. This perfect package is waterproof, color-coded, and filled with a delicious, nutritious wealth of food.

Taste and you will see that Hashem is good.

(Tehillim 34:9)

When we consider the amazing creations and all of Hashem's gifts to us, we will come to appreciate all the good that He does for us and come to love Him more and more.

The way you spend your day is an indication of what you truly love.

Chapter 52

FEAR HASHEM

In the previous chapter, we learned from the Rambam how to develop our love of Hashem. The Rambam continues and tells us how to come to fear Hashem. He says that by contemplating Hashem's ways even further, by considering that Hashem gave us life and sustains us, we will also come to fear Hashem.

Life is the greatest gift and we love Hashem for it, but we also need to be fearful that we might lose this greatest of gifts if we don't follow Hashem's rules. The mitzvos of the Torah themselves are all gifts from Hashem, for they are guidelines for utilizing His gift of life to the maximum.

The Hebrew word for "fear," *yirah*, and the word for "see," *ro'eh*, have the same root. The eyes, which enable us to see the world, also enable us to see that Hashem, the Creator of the universe, is in control. He gave us life, and He can take it away. True fear of Hashem is derived from being aware of Him — from "seeing" His providence in this world (Rav Avigdor Miller, *Praise My Soul*, paragraph 752).

But we will only fear Him to the extent that we open our eyes to recognize that Hashem is watching us all the time. What you "see" is what you will get.

Thus, the Talmud says, "Everything is in Hashem's hands except for awe of Hashem" (*Berachos* 33b). Hashem granted us the free will to choose to be in awe of Him and to follow His mitzvos.

Those who fulfill the mitzvah of tzitzis with enthusiasm will merit to view the splendor of the Shechinah (the Divine Presence).

(*Menachos* 43b)

Tzitzis reminds us of all the mitzvos of Hashem; when we see this "uniform" of the Jew, we recall who we are and what we have to do. Through tzitzis, we will merit to "see" the greatest of rewards.

Chapter 53

SERVE HASHEM

All that you do should be done for the sake of serving Hashem.

(*Avos* 2:17)

All of these principles that we have learned — belief and trust in Hashem, love and fear of Hashem — bring us to serve Hashem in everything we do.

How do we accomplish this? The first halachah in *Shulchan Aruch Orach Chaim* begins with this great principle of Judaism: "I place Hashem before me always" (*Tehillim* 17:8). If we always act as if we are in Hashem's Presence — realizing that He is in our homes, on the streets, in the airplanes and the subways — it will impact how we conduct ourselves in every area of our lives. Every act that we do throughout the day will be a form of expressing that we want to connect with Him and serve Him in every area of our lives.

Our love and fear of Hashem is manifest in the way we see Hashem in everything we do. We realize that Hashem created us all in His image in order to bestow goodness and blessing upon us, and thus we in turn want to serve Him by studying His Torah and doing His mitzvos, by praying to Him and helping others who were created in His image.

> *Hashem saw that everything He created was very good.*
>
> (*Bereishis* 1:21)

When we follow through with our free will to choose to fulfill our purpose, we also achieve our perfection. Then Hashem will see that we, His creations, are very good!

The last words of the Holy Torah are *"l'einei kol Yisrael* — before the eyes of every Jew." We are Hashem's witnesses. He gave us His Torah, the greatest gift in the world, as the prophet Yeshayah points out (*Yeshayahu* 43:10). Our eyes should serve to teach us what it means to fulfill our mission as Jews who serve Hashem and relate His praises, as it says, "This nation I have created for Me to relate My praise" (*Yeshayahu* 43:21).

There Is No One Other Than Him

Rav Chaim Volozhiner once explained to someone that a person cannot do anything without Hashem's help. The man objected: "I can take this glass and smash it without Hashem's help!" The man threw the glass down, but it didn't break. He tried again and again, to no avail. Rav Chaim then took the glass and let it drop, and it broke immediately.

(Told by Rav Nosson Wachtfogel, *zt"l*,
No'am HaMussar)

Small Books.

TARGUM
PRESS
BOOKS

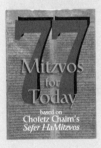